The 4ourth Floor

The 4ourth Floor

Career Counsel for Navigating the Corporate Maze

Maryam Ibrahim Al Mansoori

HAMAD BIN KHALIFA UNIVERSITY PRESS

First English edition in 2018

Hamad bin Khalifa University Press
P O Box 5825
Doha, Qatar

www.hbkupress.com

The Fourth Floor

Copyright © Maryam Ibrahim Al Mansoori, 2018
Special thanks to acclaimed photographer Khalifa Al Obaidly

All rights reserved.

No part of this publication may be reproduced or transmitted in any form or by any means, electronic or mechanical, including photocopying, recording, or any information storage or retrieval system, without prior permission in writing from the publishers.

No responsibility for loss caused to any individual or organization acting on or refraining from action as a result of the material in this publication can be accepted by HBKU Press or the author.

ISBN: 9789927119828

Qatar National Library Cataloging-in-Publication (CIP)

Mansoori, Maryam Ibrahim, author.

 The 4ourth floor : career counsel for navigating the corporate maze / Maryam Ibrahim Al Mansoori. – Doha : Hamad bin Khalifa University Press , 2018.

 Pages ; cm.

 ISBN : 978-9927-119-82-8

 1. Career management -- Qatar. II. Title.

HF5381. M36 2018

650.14-dc23   201726174868

Table of Contents

PREFACE	9
TAKE THE PLUNGE	11
LAYING THE GROUNDWORK	13
BREAKING AWAY FROM THE MOLD	15
SELF CARE 101	17
PRACTICE MAKES PERFECT	19
CLIMBING UP THE LADDER	21
GROUND ZERO	23
BE ON YOUR GAME	25
THE "ME" BRAND	27
LESS IS MORE	29
ROLE MODEL	31
WALK THE TALK	33
EMBRACE CHANGE	35
MANAGE TIME TO MANAGE SUCCESS	37
HUMAN FIRST, MANAGER SECOND	39
FINDING HUMOR IN THE HUMORLESS	41

A MOSAIC OR A MELTING POT?	43
LET GO OF WHAT YOU CAN'T CONTROL	45
KNOWING VS. UNDERSTANDING	47
SWITCH OFF	49
PUT YOUR GAME FACE ON	51
DON'T WASTE A GOOD MISTAKE	53
ACCEPTANCE OF THE OTHERS	55
DIFFERENT PERSPECTIVES MEAN DIFFERENT PRIORITIES	57
SURVIVAL OF THE FITTEST	59
THE CORPORATE CORE	61
AT THE END OF YOUR ROPE	63
THINK TWICE; ACT ONCE	65
TO LEAVE OR NOT TO LEAVE?	67
WHEN I AM GONE, …	69
ABOUT THE AUTHOR	71

PREFACE

In each one's career, there comes a unique and special experience that stays with them. It is always at hand to relate to; to hold on to. Some thoughts linger forever.

I was on the fourth floor, by virtue of my office being located there. It was a place where many stories took life, dreams grew wings, and much learning and experience was patiently, and tirelessly, gained. In that sense, it was sacred.

At different times of our lives, we are placed in different locations. The thought of writing this book came when I was stationed on this particular floor.

Without being here, I would not have thought of writing this book. The fourth floor doubled as a churn, where the seed of the book germinated and took root. For me, it was truly, and quite literally, a floor with a view.

They are a sum total of my experiences, gathered over the years while working at different organizations in various capacities.

The book is an effort to compile common thoughts, questions, and doubts that may come to a person during the course of one's career. The intent is to answer these honestly, so it may help negotiate the challenges that one may face at the workplace.

I hope that this book will serve as an eye-opener for people in the various stages of their careers. I invite you to pick a flower from the garden that first sprouted on the fourth floor, and keep it in your care, and from it, learn and grow.

TAKE THE PLUNGE

Everyone needs a job. For some, it is a simple means of livelihood, something that sustains them. And so, it must be done; even if the enthusiasm is lacking. For others, it is something tangible that drives them. It is the purpose of their lives. It is not just a job, it is a dream they live out every moment.

If your heart is not into it, it will cease to be a source of joy and satisfaction. It will become a rut out of which there is no escape.

Choose a job that stimulates you. One that allows you to innovate and flourish. Bring your passion to work. Put your heart and soul into it. Do not limit yourself to your job profile. Grow every single day. Stick to what you do best, and strive to excel in it.

If your current job is not working for you, look for one that will.

The co-founder of Apple Inc., the late Steve Jobs' passion and dedication to work was legendary. Talking about an ideal job, he said: **"The only way to do great work is to love what you do. If you have not found it yet, keep looking. Do not settle. As with all matters of the heart, you will know when you find it."**

To stop looking would be to halt your dreams midway. And that would be a pity. For dreams are there for a reason. They are what keep us going.

LAYING THE GROUNDWORK

The most critical part of a superstructure is its foundation. How strong a building is, how resilient it will be to external shocks, will be determined by its foundation.

A fragile base leads to a collapsible structure, or one that develops cracks easily. It will crumble away. To withstand the vagaries of external pressure, the core must be solid, and dug deep into the earth.

It works the same way for individuals. A well-fortified personality is a result of a foundation that is built on a strong value system. You will emerge as one with a robust character if you are well-rooted. You will not succumb to pressure, and will not be easily disturbed or affected. That is how people who can endure are produced.

"**The loftier the building**," author Thomas à Kempis wrote, "**the deeper must the foundation be laid.**" Its importance cannot be undermined.

Professionally, too, it is true. Management, for example, is a multi-disciplinary approach that requires experience and skills in different areas. It will be of immense help if your bedrock is built on knowledge, experience, and confidence. Only then will you go a long way.

Either personally or professionally, a sound base makes all the difference. It will be for all to see, as it will set you apart.

BREAKING AWAY FROM THE MOLD

It is common for people to believe in certain stereotypes. All of us are guilty of it to some extent. Often, people fall a victim to preconceived notions and misjudge colleagues. It may lead them to make wrong choices. If you are a promising young intern/worker, they may let you go, skeptical of your work experience and abilities. If you are a woman, they may automatically assume you are less capable or incompetent simply because of your gender.

Of course, they are mistaken. The number of years, gender, race, and even ethnicity have no link to professional competence.

A young professional could be more knowledgeable, capable, and more exposed to the latest market trends. A woman manager may be more dynamic, hardworking, more reliable, and even more talented than the typical male manager existing in the presumptive belief system.

Old wisdom warns against judging a book by its cover, but that is not how the world works as the reality of stereotypes remains. Be mindful of the fact that you may have already been labelled as a stereotype.

Chimamanda Ngozi Adichie, celebrated Nigerian novelist, describes the problem of stereotypes, as follows: "**The problem with stereotypes is not that they are untrue, but that they are incomplete. They make one story become the only story.**"

It is for you to decide which story you want people to craft about you — whether you help them break a stereotypical image to enable you to prove yourself by virtue of a level playing field, or reinforce their belief by proving they have been right all along.

Avoid behaviors and actions that may be counterproductive to the professional image you want to portray. Widen your personal and professional achievement gap. It is in your hands to prove them right, or wrong. The ball, like they say, is in your court.

SELF CARE 101

When you are aboard a plane, you are given safety instructions that clearly indicate that in a time of an emergency, you have to first put on your own oxygen mask before assisting anyone else. This simple safety rule reiterates the fact that in any scheme of things — at home or work, in an emergency or in a normal situation — you have to be able to first help yourself before you can lend a helping hand to others. YOU are of utmost importance.

If you do not feel energized, you will not be able to enthuse others with energy. If you are not inspired, you cannot inspire others. If you are not driven, you cannot be the driving force for others.

A weak person cannot be a source of strength and motivation to anyone. If, for instance, you ignore your health and are ailing, how can you take care of your loved ones? Whether it is for your family, or your team at work, you yourself have to be strong to be a pillar of strength for others.

And no, to put yourself first, to take care of your needs first, would not amount as an act of selfishness.

Inspirational writer Eleanor Brownn emphasizes that, **"Self-care is not selfish since you cannot serve from an empty vessel."** Focus on yourself. Being there for others starts with taking good care of yourself. The time to start taking care of yourself is NOW; there is no better time than the present!

PRACTICE MAKES PERFECT

Training is a crucial aspect to reach a target. Preparedness, planning, and training go hand in hand. Training is not a month-long affair, nor a year-long project. It is an ongoing practice session — repeated day after day, week after week, month after month, and year after year.

Athlete and four-time Olympic gold medalist, Jesse Owens, nailed it with his remark: **"A lifetime of training for just ten seconds."**

Training is most certainly not a piece of cake. It is grueling, and will test your determination — much like the training akin to Everest-climbing.

The difference here being that your 'Everest' is your 'target', and the training is not the literal Everest routine. Sports training, it is said, comprises of 5 S's — stamina, speed, skill, strength, and spirit. All these are imperative in equal measure for success. You will be required to push your limits and be willing to put in the effort. Training will make you mentally agile, and physically less prone to fatigue. Practice, indeed, does make one perfect.

These principles, while sports-oriented, are relevant and akin to training at the workplace — as vital in the professional turf, as on the field. Adopting these will ensure a steady career progression.

"We are what we repeatedly do," stated the wise Aristotle, **"excellence, therefore, is not an act but a habit."**

Get in your training gear and get moving—the target will be within easy reach.

CLIMBING UP THE LADDER

Everyone dreams of an impressive career, one which is fulfilling and stimulating at the same time. Being ambitious or career-minded is a good thing. Perhaps the only thing to be mindful of is to give it time. Do not be in a tearing rush to reach greater heights. Career progression is a gradual process. Set realistic goals for yourself. Take the stairs, not the elevator.

"**Progress lies not in enhancing what is**," said writer-poet Kahlil Gibran, "**but in advancing towards what will be**."

Remember, you have to run your own race, so choose a comfortable pace that will not burn you out. Packing in far too much in too little time will diminish your enthusiasm, until it is all but extinguished. Before long, your zeal will dissipate and your interest will wane.

No one starts right at the top. A General must first start out as a foot soldier. A CEO must first work a standard desk job. A motor vehicle first runs on gear 1 before slowly easing into higher gears. The milestones along the way are crucial—milestones of experience, of learning, of committing to memory the lessons, the wisdom, pushing yourself hard, but knowing when to slow down, and when to pause.

You are your car. How you drive it will decide where, how and in what condition it gets you to the destination of your choice. Whether it is a bumpy ride or a smooth cruise, it is your decision to make.

GROUND ZERO

Every journey begins with the first step, often one that is hesitant and unsure. One step leads to another. The process begins with gradual steps, which with time and experience, become steady. Familiarize yourself with your surroundings, become attuned to the new work environment, and get comfortable.

A runner summed up his marathon years below:

**At mile 20, I thought I was dead.
At mile 22, I wished I was dead.
At mile 24, I knew I was dead.
At mile 26.2, I realized I had become too tough to kill.**

There is a lesson here; one that applies to both our life and career. Baby steps are key. This is especially true when taking up a new job.

Remember the age-old hare-tortoise tale? Do not be in a frantic haste to cross the finishing line. Realize, it is no race, there is no finishing line, only a notional limit that gets pushed away just as it is within easy reach. The goal is not the finish line. It is learning, assimilating, imbibing a belief system along the path that leads to the general direction of the finishing line and gaining confidence and experience along the way.

When we take up a new job, we show a lot of enthusiasm in order to prove ourselves. But you should not overdo it. It may not be possible to sustain such high levels of enthusiasm in the long run. You may ease up and find yourself returning to your natural pace with the passage of time. But the expectations of your colleagues will have gone up. The change would be perceived in a negative light, even though you are doing your best.

Keep it real. Running a marathon requires training in how to save your energy at the start and accelerating slowly to reach the end. The same is true of your objectives. Do not burn yourself out instantly, as there is a whole life ahead of you.

BE ON YOUR GAME

Be in step with the times. Staying too far back into the past is detrimental to growth—both personally and professionally. Do not remain stuck in a time warp, for old ways will not push open new doors.

To make way for the new, be flexible. Rigidity will restrict and confine you. It will draw boundaries, and also close you in. A successful person is one who will not be defined by such parameters nor intimidated by challenges. One who embraces the present, and eagerly awaits to learn what the future have to offer.

Life is a continuous learning process. It is when you stop learning that you also cease to evolve. You may be brilliant in your work, but do not let complacency set in. Do not rest on your past laurels. Upgrade your existing skills, and develop new ones. Make the best use of technology; do not let it intimidate you. Work on smarter, quicker methods to do what would traditionally take long hours.

Think of the new possibilities that the present times throw up.

Do not resist change. As per a Chinese proverb,"**when the winds of change blow, some people build walls, others build windmills**." Are you the one who laments the loss of the 'good old days', or one who seizes the opportunities ushered in by the new times? Which category do you belong to?

THE "ME" BRAND

A brand is everything for a company. It is what instils confidence in the market; it is what makes a consumer choose one product over the other. It is, in a nutshell, the quintessence of the existence of a company.

Similarly, think of yourself as a brand. You are unique. This confidence is essential. While overconfidence is a negative trait, and must be avoided, the absence of confidence in yourself altogether will do no good either. A low self-esteem, or an inferiority complex, is a potential recipe for failure. Do not dilute your value. Do not underestimate yourself, or your worth.

"**Your brand**," says Jeff Bezos, CEO and founder of Amazon, "**is what other people say about you when you are not in the room.**"

Treat 'Brand Me' as any other product on offer in the market. It must have value proposition, differentiation strategy and communication, and marketing plans.

This kind of brand building, or personal development, does not come easy. It takes years to nurture. It will require sweat, toil, tears, sheer grit, and consistency. After all, you are creating a formidable reputation. And you — above all — have to persevere and contribute toward its growth. All of the effort has to come from you.

A track record of achievements, successes, and qualifications are integral to your brand portfolio which lend credibility to what you are marketing. Being different by acquiring new skills that are uncommon will add to your development. Once you have succeeded in achieving it, and treat yourself as a precious brand that must be safeguarded, chances are others will share your opinion, too.

Pause to consider: What sort of a brand do you wish to create for yourself? What do you want to be known for?

LESS IS MORE

The more you talk, the more you expose yourself. Sometimes, your ignorance may reveal itself. At other times, your unflattering qualities could surface. In the absence of not giving your speech a thought, there is always the possibility of blurting out unwanted remarks. Some loose comments, even if inadvertent, may cause you embarrassment while others could leave someone else squirming in social situations or in the workplace. Unbridled enthusiasm could do more harm than good.

Talking a lot often results in losing the thread of the conversation. The focus is lost, with thoughts going everywhere. Least said, soonest mended — the more 'mindful' you are of what you are saying, the better the chances are that you won't need damage control or, if necessary, it will be minimal.

Speak less, and learn when to be silent. Develop good listening skills. These are part of effective communication.

Speech is silver but silence is gold. Words are powerful. Weigh your words, and their meaning. If you have something substantial to contribute to a conversation, do so. If the points you wish to make seem irrelevant, or are out of context, it would be a good idea to hold yourself back.

People who talk less are often successful and accomplish more. Such people are respected for their opinion. Because of their limited words, when they do choose to speak, they are taken seriously. The less people think, the more they talk, goes a proverb. Give it a thought.

ROLE MODEL

We often hear about role models, and stories of how they influenced and inspired individuals — even societies. Is a role model necessary? Does it help to have an icon or someone to look up to?

Irish novelist Oliver Goldsmith believed **"People seldom improve if they have no other model but themselves to copy."** It may be true.

Be it a public figure, or a more personal idol at home or work, some people evoke respect for what they are, and what they stand for. It, therefore, becomes incumbent on a public personality to conduct himself/herself responsibly, and with dignity.

While selecting a role model, be cautious who you choose, and for what qualities. Do not limit yourself to just one role model. Just like when you shop, you pick the best stuff and, at times, mix and match for a more fulfilling experience.

Likewise, for the qualities you wish to inculcate in yourself — select the traits, behaviors, skills, and styles you seek to embody.

Choose from among different people. No one is perfect; everyone has flaws which means that no one person will possess all the qualities you aspire to cultivate for yourself. Not everyone is worthy of emulation. Do not restrict your vision.

"I think that the biggest role models are people that have maybe struggled and then finally gotten to their destination," said the late American actor and youth icon, Jonathan Brandis.

A role model is meant to inspire. Keep your individuality intact as you take on new personality attributes. Do not lose yourself.

WALK THE TALK

It is a universal truth that it is easier said than done. Talking the talk comes easy. The real challenge is walking the walk. It is the ability to let actions and performance speak for themselves. The one who is able to lead by example is truly respected and admired as a leader.

Demonstrate, do not explain.

Benjamin Franklin, one of the founding fathers of the United States of America, said: "**Well done is better than well said.**" Be the example you want others to follow. If you seek respect, you must offer it first. It is a two-way street. Respect begets respect, which is true of all other values, too. You not only have to earn it, you must also show it to others.

If you are seen as someone who struggles with showing respect for others, but want it for yourself, you will lose the moral authority to expect it of others. Similarly, if you want people to put in a certain number of work hours, you must lead by example and work those many yourself, if not more. You will see how contagious it is.

Mere words serve no purpose. You have to walk the path yourself if you want your words to carry weight and meaning. And then, there will be nothing left to say. Actions will always speak louder than words.

EMBRACE CHANGE

Yes, good bosses do exist. They are not a figment of imagination, like the mythical, one-horned unicorn. For every uninspiring boss out there, there is an equally real and humane boss who wants to bring out the best in his colleagues.

American author and speaker John C. Maxwell defines a good boss as a person "**…who takes a little more than his share of the blame, and a little less than his share of the credit.**" And if such bosses were to leave, it would be a heart-breaking experience. It is natural that you feel lost when you lose a mentor, a friend, philosopher, and guide — a person who helped you grow, gave you wings. This may propel you to reconsider following a favorite boss to a new destination.

If you lose a good boss, take a moment to reflect before deciding to jump ship and follow them to their new job. While this may have been a good professional move for them, it may not be so for you.

Take a moment to reflect on and mourn the loss of a good boss, but realize that the development may not be so bad.

Life has a way to push you forth, to give you what you deserve. Try to look at the opportunities that may come along. You have a chance of emerging out of the shadow. Spread your wings wider. The change in organization may actually be good for your professional growth.

Though at first, it may seem unsettling to work under a new boss, perceive it as a chance to put to work all the experience and knowledge gained under the previous boss. Armed with this confidence, embrace the new conditions at work, and find your feet. Step out of your comfort zone and prove yourself. You already have a head-start as you are still in your familiar environment. Before long, you will adjust to the new situation, and maybe even move forward within the organization.

A person does not have to be physically present to inspire. You can continue to draw strength and inspiration from your former boss. And some day, you may have the opportunity to be the sort of boss that you so deeply admired.

MANAGE TIME TO MANAGE SUCCESS

The most crucial aspect of any work, in fact, of life itself, is how best you manage your time. All achievers, like everyone else, only have 24 hours in a day at their disposal. How those hours are put to use makes all the difference.

Productive people set timelines ahead of the work they undertake and chart a course of action. Abraham Lincoln once famously remarked: **"Give me six hours to chop a tree and I will spend the first hour sharpening the axe."**

Do spadework to have a clear picture of the ground realities. Set out your objectives clearly at the outset, before undertaking the essential groundwork necessary to reach your goal and meet specific targets.

Planning is an essential part of time management. French writer Antoine de Saint-Exupéry emphasized that "**A goal without a plan is just a wish.**" If the implementation is poor, it will all fall flat.

Plan out your objectives. Prioritize and focus on areas that need your personal attention while delegating other less important matters. The energy at work is contagious, much like a yawn. So, be mindful of the personal energy you bring to work. Decision-making, enthusiasm, clarity, efficiency, and positivity all combined define energy.

A Harvard Business Review study says personal energy comes from four main sources: the body, the emotions, the mind, and the spirit. Through a conscious effort, this energy can be revived, and expanded.

Personal energy will lead to improved management of time which will reduce the duration of work through efficiency. Hence, time and energy go hand in hand.

HUMAN FIRST, MANAGER SECOND

An essential lesson in management is connecting with the team. For this, it is vital to know your team well. You should know what makes each of them tick. This awareness about their mental state and emotional well-being is crucial, and should concern you. Any personal conflict can take a toll on the efficacy of the entire team. If you sense a problem or some distress, be quick to address it.

Be easily accessible and open up to your team. People should be willing to walk up to you to discuss their problems. You need to reinforce the confidence in them that their issues are safe with you, and will not be all over the workplace. That is the first step in confidence building. People will put their faith in you only when they know you can be trusted. The onus would be on you to not let them down. Trust takes a long, long time to build, and a very short time to lose.

"**An open heart is an open mind**," says the Dalai Lama. But while you connect with the team at an emotional level, take care not to overstep the line. Some things are personal and ought to remain so. Not all may want to share their problems with you. Respect their privacy.

Also, being too close can sometimes blur power equations, encouraging people to take undue liberties. Guard against it. This will erode your authority, and undermine your position. Therefore, while you work on the hearts and minds of others, a sensible head over your shoulders will stand you in good stead.

FINDING HUMOR IN THE HUMORLESS

The overall environment in a workplace, ideally, should be conducive. But like most things in life, there is no way to guarantee it. It may unfold positively for you, or it may be anything but encouraging to your personal and professional growth. Do not let this cause you stress. Some aspects are in your control, others are not. Accept them and look to overcome them with a positive and humorous attitude.

You can joke about the negative factors — an undeserving, or a silly boss, for example. A boss who got this far due to connections or by constantly flattering their superiors. Is it worth your time to brood about it? Certainly not. Have a hearty laugh. You can put that time to better use by focusing on your growth and skills.

Rigid co-worker? You can make light of the inflexible approach. Shrug it off. Mulling over it will not help, nor will it change the situation. Focus on enhancing the quality of your personal work experience.

In other words, learn to go with the flow. Be flexible. Bend, but not to break. "**Every time you find some humor in a difficult situation, you win**," exclaimed Peanuts comic strip illustrator, Charles M. Schulz. It cannot be truer.

A MOSAIC OR A MELTING POT?

A team is a collaboration of many minds, made possible through cooperation, and the varied skills that each team member brings along. For this reason, how well-coordinated a team is will also determine how successful it is. There is no room for 'I' here; a team is the essence of 'we' and 'us'. The goals are shared, and everyone pitches in to achieve the desired objectives. Failure and success are equally owned by all. Like American author Helen Keller said: **"Alone we can do so little, together we can do so much."**

To put together a competent team is a challenge. It is essential that the focus remains on individual skills, talents, and abilities rather than gender, specific background, or nationality. Be mindful of such preconceived biases that may be the result of a misinterpretation of previously held beliefs. These have no place in a healthy work environment.

Skills and knowledge are not confined to stereotypes. These can be found anywhere. Have a discerning eye and ear. Like a jeweler, choose your gems.

Hiring a diverse mix of capabilities will stimulate the efficiency of the team, leading to a feeling of collective pride, and better results. Such a team is an asset to any organization, which should be a melting pot of ideas — no matter who the source: a man or a woman, a native or a foreigner.

"If you want to go fast, go alone", goes an African proverb. **"But if you want to go far, go together."** A well-drawn team will take the organization there.

LET GO OF WHAT YOU CAN'T CONTROL

Some things, people, and situations cannot be changed and what cannot be changed must be endured. Try as one might, somethings cannot be altered, be it on a personal or professional front. These may relate to inflexible people, rigid situations or unforeseen circumstances. Some things must endured.

That is to say that there are, and always will be outside forces that are out of your control. And sometimes these uncontrollable forces are actually people that you have to deal with on a regular basis in the workforce. Can you change them? Most probably not: they may be people in superior positions to you, or they may be people who you are in charge of, but who are inflexible and stuck in their ways.

Know this: you cannot remodel people or get rid of them any more than you can swim against the current. It simply is not possible. You cannot change how people treat you, or their views, in an instant. Do not overly stress yourself about transforming people or changing their opinions/beliefs. It could take a lot of time and concerted effort, and may still ultimately result in failure.

What you can do is alter how you react to them. That is well within your power and control. **"What is to give light must endure burning,"** said renowned psychiatrist, Dr. Viktor Frankl.

And so while you are at it, use contrary views and 'difficult' people to evolve yourself in a positive manner and gain new skills and insights. Let them be the catalyst that triggers within you the will to excel and improve yourself — both as a professional and as a human being. Do not expend your energy in fighting a losing battle, or one that will demand a lot of your personal time. Use that energy, instead, to work on advancing your own growth.

KNOWING VS. UNDERSTANDING

Reading is easy, what is difficult is to truly understand and grasp the essence of what you have read. Once you achieve that, how best you translate that knowledge into action that would benefit you, and the place you work for, will be the challenge.

Speech is easy, too, what is tricky is to follow it up with action that is in sync with the information gathered from reading. Loose comments, boastful statements and pompous assertions are rendered meaningless in the absence of clarity in action.

It is important to understand people, too. Just as you focus on your words, tune your mind to what others have to say. Do not get immediately taken in by people. Do not trust them blindly. Allow yourself time to know them first. Trust, if deserved, can then follow.

It is therefore vital to understand that speech and action are correlated. Speech alone is unconvincing unless it is followed by a perceived application of thought and effective action.

Being intellectual and articulate are impressive attributes in an individual, but if you cannot comprehend the substance of what you have learnt and reveal it through your actions, all of the knowledge that you possess is useless. There is no practical or real use for that information.

In-depth understanding of a situation is gauged and often tested on the cornerstone of the prompt action or decision that succeeds it. Mere talk is bluster and inconsequential. Remember the saying **"Easier said than done."** To be taken seriously, you have to constantly prove and practice what you say.

SWITCH OFF

In today's high-stress world, it is important to switch off from time to time. This will not only help rejuvenate the spirit and encourage clarity, but also infuse you with a feeling of calm and wellness.

Digital detox should not be an option that is exercised by other people, but a go-to choice for you. Gadgets are ruling our lives. There is too much noise. Put that phone away for a day.

Our minds are constantly being bombarded with information and gory images. Put aside the newspaper or magazine. Do not think. Cut yourself off from the humdrum of everyday life. Connect with yourself. Relax by making place for 'me time'. Start reading the book that you never got around to reading because you never had the time. Go to the gym and exercise; something you always said you would do if you had more time.

The fact is that there never will be such more time. You simply have to make time for things that help you de-stress. Catch up with old friends and organize family dinners. Or simply laze around, doing nothing all day. These are all effective stress-busters.

Work is meant for the workplace. Do not carry it home. Any tension at the office, should be left exactly there. Brooding about the office at home could directly affect family ties, making matters worse. Your home should be sacred. Approach work-related issues at the workplace with a refreshed mind.

A well-rested mind is indeed productive. Like writer Paulo Coelho says: "**A field that has rested gives a bountiful crop.**"

PUT YOUR GAME FACE ON

In every walk of life, you will encounter rivals. Wherever there is a clash of interest, rivalry is certain to follow. Be prepared, remain watchful, and do not let your guard drop.

The most important thing is to identify your rivals. They could be people at work who directly hinder your professional growth, and set up hurdles in your path to slow you down, or simply the seemingly harmless, ever-smiling colleague — sweet to your face — but the first to throw you under the bus when you are not around. Much like what Shakespeare said: **"That one may smile, and smile, and be a villain."**

It could be a vindictive subordinate, an envious peer, or a rigid boss who hesitates to give you your due. Do not succumb to their charms, and wily tricks. Understand what makes them tick, and assess their weaknesses, which you can use to your advantage to further your own interest.

But as you stay vigilant, do not block your mind. It is said of politics that there are no permanent friends, and no permanent enemies. It is true of life, too. You may team up with a rival on a project, only to realize you had misread them. Your boss may have seemed overly harsh and inflexible, but then gave you a good appraisal. Yes, be wary and tread with caution, but be open to setting aside rivalries and negative feelings while working with people. Remember, it takes two people to be enemies.

If you can rise above animosity, you will also move ahead.

DON'T WASTE A GOOD MISTAKE

Life is a series of experiences: some good, some bad, and some in between. It is also about mistakes, wrong choices, and a lapse of judgement. No matter how many books one may have read, how scholarly one may be, real experiences come from life itself; from both failure and success. Win some, lose some, but there is always some takeaway, something gained — a lesson to be learned.

"From error to error", Freud believed, **"one discovers the entire truth."** Do not strive to be a perfectionist, rather understand that, like change, mistakes are inevitable even as you give your hundred percent.

Things will work sometimes, other times not. And in both circumstances, a keen learner will observe, take notes and move on, enriched from that experience or miscalculation.

Through trial and error most things were discovered and arrived at by scientists, researchers, and academicians. So as you move on in years and grow on the job, you will inevitably make and learn from the mistakes that you make.

The key is not to be disheartened following failure, or go over the top with success. Both extremes can be debilitating to an individual's growth, just as both are needed in equal measure for a well-rounded, holistic personality.

Embrace all kinds of experiences, acknowledge, and discuss the mistakes you make, taking comfort in the fact that in each is a life lesson.

ACCEPTANCE OF THE OTHERS

No two individuals are the same. Choices, objectives, thought processes, and life goals vary from person to person. Everyone's world view is shaped by their experiences and environment. What is right for one, may not be so for the other. This is also what makes the social ecosystem organic, otherwise it would be an assembly line at work.

Management rules are there for a reason, yes. They are basic guidelines, but not necessarily the rule of thumb for each and every situation. Feel free to twist them, and, if need be, circumvent them to make the most of a situation.

But at the same time, don't try to change people to fit into your scheme of things, or their job profiles. People do not belong in molds. Identify their strengths and use them in a way that yields the best results.

"**The job of a professional manager**," advised the renowned management consultant Peter Drucker, "**is not to like people. It is not to change people. It is to put their strengths to work.**"

Develop on the basic building block. Create and build rather than destroy. Harness qualities and personality traits that come naturally to people and are intrinsic. Something that is imposed or out of character cannot be sustained over long periods of time.

DIFFERENT PERSPECTIVES MEAN DIFFERENT PRIORITIES

If you thought you were done with school principals, authoritative figures and bosses, you now have the Board of Directors to contend with. And it is a challenge at that. Keep in mind that the Board of Directors does not necessarily share the same priorities as you, or even your enthusiasm on various issues.

The larger picture works for them; the bird's-eye view of a project, or a proposition. The nitty-gritty is your lot to handle. **"There is no magic in magic, it is all in the details,"** believed Walt Disney. Rightly so. But, more often than not, the Board of Directors may not be interested in the details. It does not have that kind of time or eye for details. That is left to you. Matters that may be of interest and importance to you, may be inconsequential to the Board of Directors.

This is not restricted to Board members alone. There is a hierarchy in every workplace, where functions, responsibilities, and priorities are carefully delineated. For instance, in a newsroom, or a publishing house, a sub-editor and, say, an associate editor cannot be expected to share the same priorities. This should not discourage you, rather step up your game and learn to deal with it. Understand how the Board of Directors functions, and perceives issues. Work your way around it. At the same time, it would be useful to connect with some people in top management by working on common goal or shared personal interest. You can take things forward from there. Positive networking and making the right connections can go a long way.

As you focus on the project, ensure that you do not lose sight of either the details or the bigger picture. Both are inter-dependent. For you, both are crucial and must exist simultaneously.

SURVIVAL OF THE FITTEST

The key to survival is but naturally the will to survive, more so, in a hostile environment. All your life skills will be put to test. This is true of the workplace as well, where, as per a Gallup study, people do not leave jobs, they leave managers. The survey of 7,200 adults found that about half had left a job at some point to get away from their manager. In effect, a bad boss is one of the top reasons for employees to quit.

In such circumstances, it is imperative to evolve a strategy and develop immunity against any negative campaign that may be directed by the boss towards you. Muster courage and focus on ways to get around a difficult boss. Have a team of like-minded colleagues who share similar views and can support you if a situation so arises.

There is strength in unity, goes the old adage. Use it to your advantage. The one thing you must actively fight against and be mindful about is your isolation. You cannot go solo on this. It would not be easy to take on your boss alone. Build connections, lobby, cultivate sources; anything that will have some people in your corner.

At the same time, do not provoke problems. Handle any confrontation with a calm mind. Try to prevent difficult situations from flaring up. Above all, do not lose heart. It could be frustrating, but good tactical and social skills can salvage any bad situation. Do not be impulsive and throw away the job. This is self-destructive and self-defeating.

"It is not the strongest of the species that survive," said Charles Darwin, "**nor the most intelligent, but the one most responsive to change.**" Adapt to change. Go with the flow. But when push comes to shove, brace yourself and have your core team ready.

THE CORPORATE CORE

Like countries, all organizations have a unique and distinctive culture. All organizations, in all fields, have a set of unstated rules and protocol that must be followed in spirit. Lou Gerstner, a former Chairman of the Board, IBM, asserts: **"Culture is not just one aspect of the game — it is the game. In the end, an organization is nothing more than the collective capacity of its people to create value."**

Success comes through only when the organization along with all its employees together march forward with a collective objective and well-coordinated efforts. Much like a vehicle with 4x4 drive: if one wheel doesn't perform well, it will impact the overall performance of the vehicle as a whole. In the absence of common objectives, full potential will not be reached — neither of the company as an entity nor the individual's.

Ensure that your professional expectations and value system are in sync with the organization. A shared professional culture and ethics are paramount for a truly satisfying work experience, as it inspires you to give your best and be on the top of your game.

You may be supremely skilled and competent, but if your value system does not match with that of the organization, you may feel like a misfit — a jigsaw puzzle piece that does not quite fit. In case you find it challenging to match the company's pace, give it careful thought. If this is a fallout of some differences with colleagues or bosses, try to remove these.

Once that is done, if you still feel out of step, it probably means you are. You should then take stock of the situation and consider a switch. Look for a company that best fits your ideals and work goals. Like a well-conducted orchestra, the rhythm must match.

AT THE END OF YOUR ROPE

We all encounter monsters in our daily lives. The monster, in this context, could be a senior colleague, the boss, or even a project or a task at hand.

"Everyone is someone's devil," according to renowned business consultant Matthew Hicks.

How to deal with this devil is a challenge no doubt, but not impossible. The first step would naturally be to identify the devil. The second would be to know your level of tolerance, and patience. How much can/will you take? If it is a short-term challenge, or something/someone that you can manage to keep at bay, you have it under control. If, on the other hand, it is something that can damage you and have long-term repercussions, it makes sense to have a strategy in place.

If a project brings along too much negative stress, or misery that will affect you physically, mentally and professionally, it is best to politely refuse to take it up, or move on. If it will bring in rewards and professional credit, deal with it tactfully. If not, it will be advisable to give it a complete pass.

If it is a drain on your health, or will have an adverse impact on your family life, it is certainly not worth hanging on to. Some things can be recovered, but good family ties and health, for example, are not recovered easily . It is beneficial to constantly weigh the challenge vis-à-vis its worth and consequences.

THINK TWICE; ACT ONCE

Decision making is a crucial aspect of life and any job. Every now and then, you will be faced with sticky situations that will test your patience, and your ability to make sound decisions with no, or minimum collateral damage.

You may find yourself in ambiguous situations where you are pushed toward taking an impulsive decision. Do not be tempted to rush in. The decision may offer temporary relief, but bring in its wake permanent regret. Any decision that is taken on the spur of the moment, without considering the repercussions, will be counterproductive. You will only regret the fallout. It will be a case of panicking under a stressful situation; buckling under pressure.

Do not let the situation get out of hand. The virtue of patience has stood the test of time. To be in control, take a decision with a calm and collected mind. It will go a long way. During stormy times, take a decision that has been well thought-out, taking into account all related factors. Sleep on it, if you have to. Take a day, or two, to arrive at a decision. Let the storm blow over and the dust settle. Only then will a clarity of vision emerge. A hazy picture will yield an equally hazy result.

Drawing on his experiences, former US President Woodrow Wilson had proclaimed: **"One cool judgement is worth a thousand hasty counsels."**

Bear in mind at all times the simple wisdom — **"Great haste makes great waste."**

TO LEAVE OR NOT TO LEAVE?

Bosses can be intimidating. According to a research, most employees who are dissatisfied leave their boss and not their organization. In the absence of a rapport with a boss, it is a fairly common practice among people to simply quit, without first assessing the situation. They choose to leave rather than stick around to deal with a particularly unaccommodating boss.

Sometimes, the pressure is too immense to withstand, compelling an employee to put in their papers. If faced with a similar situation, be prudent. Ensure that, in hindsight, it is not a decision you take in haste, only to later regret it.

Before quitting, ask yourself: Am I leaving my boss or the organization? If the answer is the former, it would be wise to reconsider the move. If your organization is conducive to your professional growth; if it has a promising future; if it allows you opportunities to tap your potential to the fullest, you must review your decision.

Author Stephen Covey nailed it when he stated: "**The main thing is to keep the main thing the main thing.**" The main thing here is to not put your boss before your aspirations. Do not be bullied. Bosses will come, bosses will go, so do not let go. You cannot cut your nose to spite your face, as they say. It will be debilitating to your progress. The loss would not be of the boss or of the company, but yours alone.

WHEN I AM GONE, ...

Whether one is an employee or a boss, there is always room to leave behind a legacy. It could be the sheer volume of work achieved under your watch, the many success stories you scripted, your impeccable track record, ceaseless integrity, the unprecedented enthusiasm that you got along in the organization, anything at all that stands out.

All things of value are rare. Qualities that are seldom seen are the ones to aspire for. These are not commonplace, and hence these are the only ones worthy of being followed as a legacy; to be left behind as one.

Do you want to leave an indelible mark, long after you have left an organization? If yes, actively work towards it. It does not come easy. It takes years and years of hard work to build, much like a lifetime achievement award.

Do you believe that people want to emulate you? Do they respect and admire you for your value system and work ethics? Do you inspire them enough for them to want to follow in your footsteps? If the answer is yes, then you have left a legacy.

Peter Strople, 'the most connected man in America' who mentors and works to bring business and community leaders together, believes that **"legacy is not leaving something 'for' people, it's leaving something 'in' people."**

In that sense legacy, is an organic entity which lives on. What do you want to be remembered for?

It Does Not End Here

As we walk through the myriad that is the corporate maze, we often hit roadblocks which can be turned into opportunities simply by tweaking our mindset on how to approach them positively.

As TS Elliot said: '**The journey, not the destination matters**…'

Make the journey count.

ABOUT THE AUTHOR

Maryam Ibrahim Al-Mansoori, a management consultant, has worked in several senior managerial positions in numerous major companies within various industries, enriching her with a profound understanding of the corporate culture.

She has, during the span of her impressive career, excelled professionally, leading strategic projects such as the design of new corporate governance framework, organization restructuring, and business process improvements, to name a few. Her portfolio is an engaging spectrum ranging from company-wide strategy, corporate planning, quality and excellence, risk management, to human resources, and information technology.

She has an Executive MBA from HEC Paris; certified in Corporate Governance from INSEAD Business School; PHR Certification from Society of Human Resource Management; and is a graduate from Qatar Leadership Center's Executives Leaders' program.

Maryam is a proficient troubleshooter and a critical thinker, making her an inspiring mentor to young talent.

She is a free spirit who keenly explores the world around her. She has been pursuing diverse interests like photography and art, and has cultivated a focused literary mind. Besides being a creative writer, she is a motivational speaker and an enthusiastic supporter of entrepreneurs.